CAN YOU CATCH A FALLING STAR?

A Question of Science Book

CAN YOU CATCH A FALLING STAR?

by Sidney Rosen
illustrated by Dean Lindberg

Carolrhoda Books, Inc. / Minneapolis

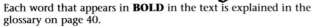

Each word that appears in **BOLD** in the text is explained in the glossary on page 40.

For metric conversion: when you know the number of miles, multiply by 1.61 to find the correct number of kilometers. When you know the number of tons, multiply by .9 to find the correct number of metric tons.

Text copyright © 1995 by Sidney Rosen
Illustrations copyright © 1995 by Carolrhoda Books, Inc.
Photographs reproduced courtesy of: Science Graphics, cover, p. 20; Hal Povenmire, Florida Fireball Patrol, pp. 2–3, 4–5, 38–39; Lunar and Planetary Institute, pp. 7, 29; NASA, pp. 8, 11, 16, 25, 28, 33, 36; © Mr. & Mrs. James M. Baker, Lillian, AL, p. 9; Courtesy Department Library Services, American Museum of Natural History, pp. 10 (Neg. #45634. Photo by J. Otis Wheelock.), 34 (Neg. #45085. Photo by Orchard.); © Robert C. Mitchell, p. 19; © Terence Dickinson, p. 23; Don Haar, pp. 31, 32.

Carolrhoda Books, Inc. c/o The Lerner Group
241 First Avenue North, Minneapolis, MN 55401

LIBRARY OF CONGRESS CATALOGING-IN-PUBLICATION DATA

Rosen, Sidney.
   Can you catch a falling star? / by Sidney Rosen ; illustrated by Dean Lindberg.
      p. cm. — (A Question of science book)
   ISBN 0-87614-882-8
   1. Meteors—Miscellanea—Juvenile literature. [1. Meteors—Miscellanea. 2. Questions and answers.] I. Lindberg, Dean, ill. II. Title. III. Series.
QB741.5.R68 1995
523.5'1—dc20   94-38478
                                                              CIP
                                                              AC

Manufactured in the United States of America
1 2 3 4 5 6 – M – 00 99 98 97 96 95

How can I catch a falling star?

Hold on! Let's get one thing straight. A falling star is not a star at all.

It isn't?

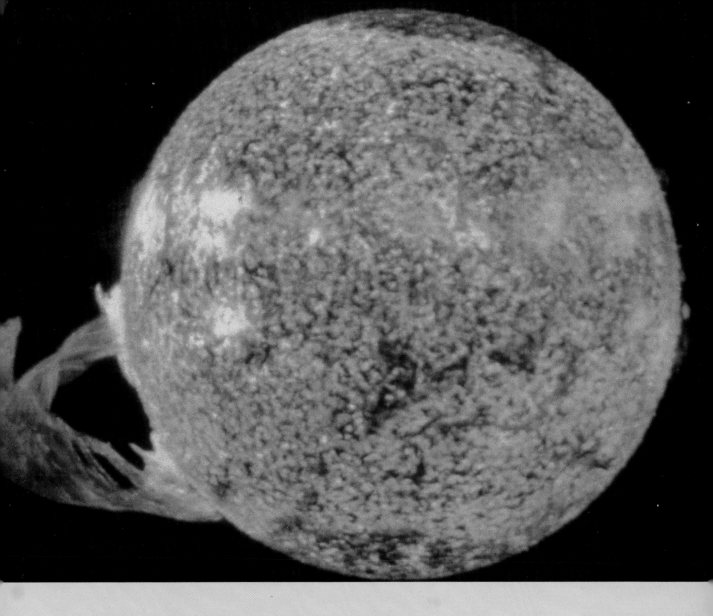

No. Stars are huge burning balls of gas. The
closest star, our Sun, is 93 million miles away.
But the trail of light you call a falling star is much
closer than that. Scientists call that light trail a
meteor. Sometimes meteors are also called
shooting stars.

If a meteor isn't a star, then what is it?

It's a piece of space junk that has just zoomed close to Earth. All around the Earth is a layer of gases called the atmosphere.

When bits of rock and dust from space hit and rub against the atmosphere, that space junk burns white-hot. You'll see a streak of white light in the sky before the space junk burns up or hits the ground.

Any part of that space junk that survives and hits the Earth is called a **meteorite**. Very large and extra-bright meteors are called fireballs.

What happens when a meteorite hits the ground?

A big meteorite can create a **crater,** a hole formed when it hits the Earth. Most meteorites are too small to make craters, but there are exceptions. The biggest meteorite ever found in the United States fell near Willamette, Washington, in 1902. It weighed about 14 tons!

Where do meteorites come from?

Most are thought to come from **comets**.

Wait a minute! Are comets and meteorites the same thing?

Not exactly. A comet is a big frozen ball of space junk that passes by the Earth on its trip from outer space. A comet moves in an **orbit** around the Sun.

What's an orbit?

That's the circle-shaped path that a smaller object follows around a larger object. The Earth orbits the Sun. Comets do, too.

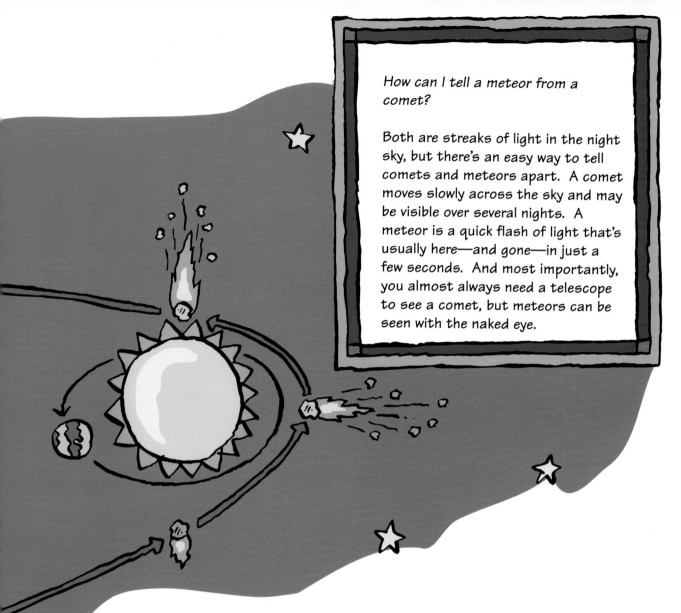

How can I tell a meteor from a comet?

Both are streaks of light in the night sky, but there's an easy way to tell comets and meteors apart. A comet moves slowly across the sky and may be visible over several nights. A meteor is a quick flash of light that's usually here—and gone—in just a few seconds. And most importantly, you almost always need a telescope to see a comet, but meteors can be seen with the naked eye.

When a comet is going around the Sun, the Sun causes part of the comet's surface to blow off. These blown-off pieces and dust move around in the **Solar System**. Some of the pieces fly into the Earth's atmosphere and become meteorites.

What happens to the ones that don't become meteorites?

They remain in space and keep moving around the Sun. Larger pieces are called **meteoroids**. That's what a piece of space junk is called before it hits the atmosphere. The very, very tiny ones are called micrometeoroids.

If they are so tiny, how do we know they are there?

They bump into the spacecraft we send up to the moon and to other planets, like Mars. In fact, all spacecraft, with or without people in them, are in danger of being hit by micrometeoroids. Special care has to be taken so that micrometeoroids cause the smallest possible damage.

How could anything that small cause damage?

Micrometeoroids are moving so fast, they could go right through the skin of a spaceship. Micrometeoroids have been clocked at speeds ranging from about 9 miles per second to about 42 miles per second!

Could the dust in my room be from a meteorite?

Are some of the falling stars we see micrometeoroids?

Probably not. Micrometeoroids are usually much too small to give off light when they hit the atmosphere. Some do make it to the Earth's surface where they become micrometeorites.

Sure! Some meteorites break down into dust particles. And micrometeorites are already as small as dust. However, it's hard to tell which bits of dust in your room come from meteorites and which come from the Earth.

Can I see meteors in the sky every night?

On clear nights, there is always a chance that you will see a meteor. But there are certain times during the year when meteor watching is best.

When is that?

One of the best times is early in the morning on August 12. That's when the Perseid meteor shower takes place.

Where did it get its name?

It's called Perseid because meteors seem to come from the part of the sky where we see a group of stars, or a **constellation**, called Perseus.

Why is it called a shower?

Have you ever tried to look right into a showerhead when the water was turned on? Think of all those streams of water as separate drops rushing at you.

That's what a shower of meteors is like. During a meteor shower, you can see hundreds of meteors flashing through the sky.

So are the Perseid meteors pieces of the stars that we see in Perseus?

When should I try to catch a falling star?

There are many meteor showers, but here are the six biggest ones. Their names will help you know where to look for them in the sky. The names in parentheses refer to the constellations from which the meteors seem to come. Showers may last several days, and the date given here is the best day for watching. Remember, the best time for watching is during the early hours before sunrise.

Eta Aquarids (Aquarius)	May 4
Perseids (Perseus)	August 12
Orionids (Orion)	October 22
Taurids (Taurus)	November 1
Leonids (Leo)	November 17
Geminids (Gemini)	December 14

No. Remember, meteors aren't stars at all. In this case, the meteors are the leftover bits of a comet. That comet came through the Solar System in 1866. Every year since then, when the Earth crosses the path of that old comet, we see a meteor shower.

What's another good time to watch for meteors?

Try watching the sky on December 14 or so. That's when the Earth runs into a group of meteors called the Geminid shower. That shower takes place early in the morning, before sunrise. The meteors seem to come out of the constellation called Gemini.

Do the Geminid meteors come from a comet?

No, they don't. **Astronomers** think they come
from a different place. These meteors are from
part of the Solar System called the **asteroid belt**.

What's the asteroid belt?

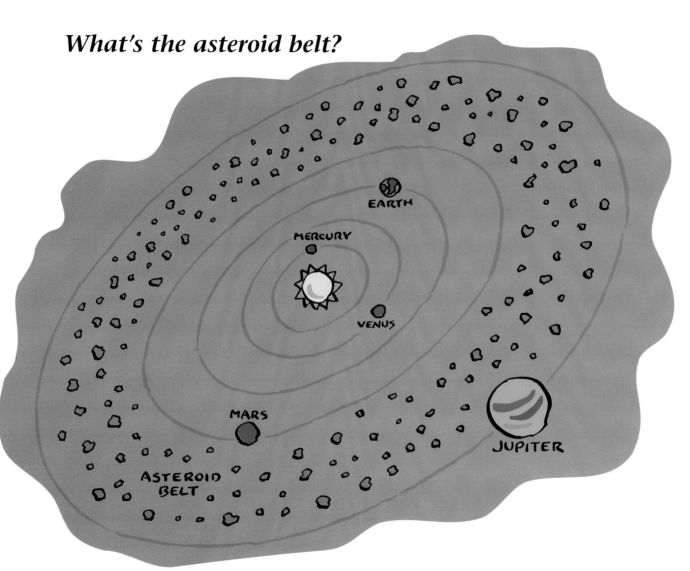

It's an area of space junk in the Solar System
between the planets Mars and Jupiter. This area
is a ring, or belt, of small rocky objects, all going
around the Sun. These objects are called **asteroids**.

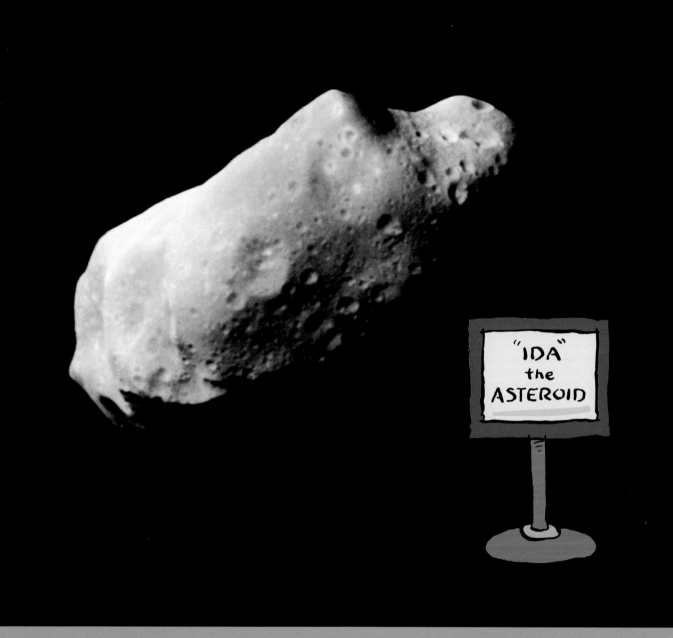

There are thousands of asteroids in the asteroid belt. Some are less than a mile across. The largest we have found, Ceres, is almost 600 miles across. It would almost cover the state of Texas!

How do asteroids become meteoroids?

The asteroid belt is like a circle-shaped freeway. Imagine a wide road with hundreds of traffic lanes all crossing each other. Thousands of cars and trucks of all sizes are speeding in the lanes. The chances of a crash are pretty good.

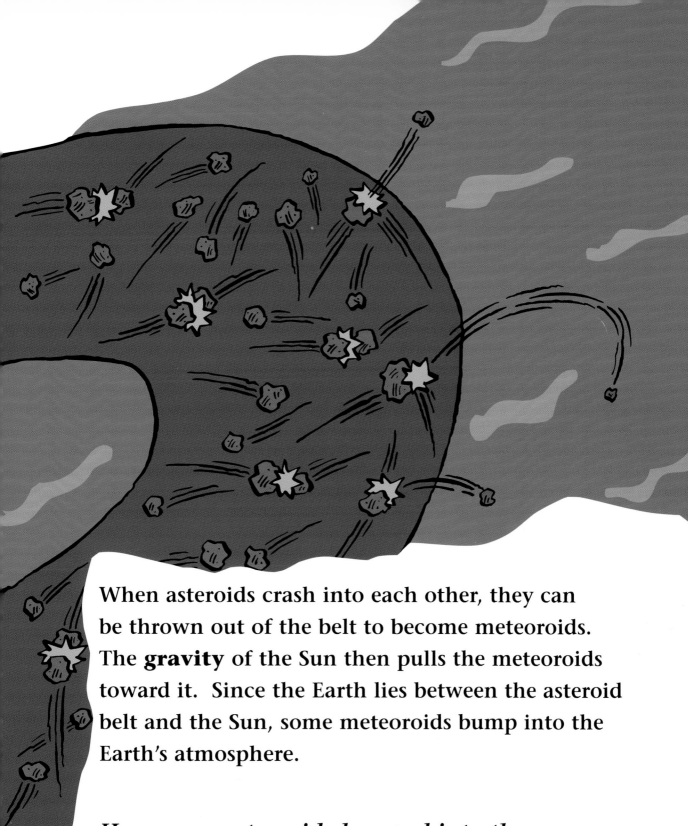

When asteroids crash into each other, they can be thrown out of the belt to become meteoroids. The **gravity** of the Sun then pulls the meteoroids toward it. Since the Earth lies between the asteroid belt and the Sun, some meteoroids bump into the Earth's atmosphere.

Have any meteoroids bumped into the moon on their way toward Earth?

Oh, boy, have they! Craters on the moon tell us
that millions of years ago, when the Solar System
was forming, the skies must have been filled with
meteoroids of all sizes.

Yikes! Some of those craters are pretty big!
Have meteorites ever made craters on Earth?

Yes, but most craters made long ago have been covered by oceans or erased by rains. Meteor Crater, in Arizona, was formed by a large meteorite and is more than a half mile across. Scientists believe this crater was formed about 25,000 years ago.

Wow, that's scary. Could a meteor come out of the sky and hit my house?

It's possible, but not very likely. There are far fewer meteorites hitting the Earth now than there were when the Earth was forming.

Only three houses in the United States are known to have been hit by meteorites in the past 50 years. These meteorites were small and did little damage. But the people in those houses sure were surprised. Wanda and Bob Donahue were watching TV when a meteorite landed in their house. Meteorites have landed twice in their hometown of Wethersfield, Connecticut!

This is the Donahues' meteorite. It's called
Wethersfield II.

*But that meteorite looks just like a rock. How
can you tell a meteorite from a rock?*

Sometimes you can't. But the more you know
about meteorites, the easier it will be. Meteorite
hunters know that there are three major types of
meteorites.

Some look just like Earth rocks. They are called stones. They are the most common type of meteorite but the hardest to find. Not only do they look like ordinary rocks, but they also wear away quickly. If you don't see it fall, you may never find a stone.

I'm called a stone and I may look like an ordinary rock, but I come from outer space!

The easiest meteorites to find and recognize are called irons. They contain pure iron, something never found in Earth rocks. Meteorite hunters use magnets and metal detectors to look for irons. Stony-irons, the third kind of meteorite, are a mixture of stone and iron.

Where's the best place on Earth to go hunting for meteorites?

Almost anywhere. Of course, it's easier to spot stones that might be meteorites in open country—like deserts or beaches—without covering grass. Most recently, a number of meteorites have been found in the ice and snow of Antarctica. Meteorites stand out nicely against the white ground. Make sure you're dressed as warm as a polar bear if you head in that direction.

Scientists are always on the lookout for stones, irons, stony-irons, and certain special meteorites.

Why are they special?

Because they come from unusual places. This one
probably came from Mars.

EETA79001

Astronomers believe that long ago pieces of the
moon and of Mars must have been broken off
when meteorites hit them. Those pieces in turn
became meteorites here on Earth.

So what does that prove?

How can a meteorite tell us about the early years of the Solar System?

Some meteorites are over four billion years old. Written out, that's 4,000,000,000! Scientists believe that these meteorites came from asteroids or planets that were around when the Solar System was very young. Of course, just knowing how old the meteorites are doesn't tell us how the Solar System was formed. But by studying the chemical elements in meteorites, we can learn something about the chemicals that combined to form the planets, moons, asteroids, and Sun.

Just as a detective uses clues to solve a mystery, astronomers use what meteorites tell them to solve the mystery of how the Solar System was formed.

So can I catch a falling star and be a detective, too?

Your chances of finding a meteorite are pretty small. Most burn up before they reach the ground. But your chances will be better if you get up very early in the morning.

How's that?

Go outside. You probably won't catch a falling star, but you might catch a glimpse of a beautiful meteor streaking across the sky!

GLOSSARY

asteroid belt: The region of space between the orbits of Mars and Jupiter

asteroids: Several thousand small, rocky bodies orbiting the Sun between the orbits of Mars and Jupiter

astronomers: Scientists who are interested in explaining how the universe works and who observe and study the planets, stars, and galaxies for this purpose

comets: Frozen pieces of space rock and dust that come from outside the Solar System and orbit the Sun

constellation: One of a number of patterns of fixed stars in the sky that are often named after animals, gods, or mythical heroes

crater: A circle-shaped hollow caused by the impact of meteors and other objects hitting the surface of the Earth, moon, or other planets

gravity: The force that makes objects attract each other. The Earth's gravity is so strong it keeps us stuck to Earth.

meteor: A hot, glowing object that flashes through the Earth's atmosphere

meteorite: A solid body that gets through the Earth's atmosphere without burning up and falls to the ground

meteoroids: Small bodies in space that orbit the Sun

orbit: The path of one object around another, such as the moon around the Earth

Solar System: The Sun and all the bodies that move around it—planets, moons, comets, asteroids, and meteors

DATE DUE

MAR 25			
SEP			
OCT			
SEP 10			
JUL 1 2 2011			